JAPANESE

COOKING

FOR TWO

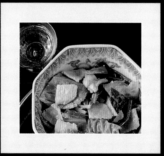

JAPANESE
COOKING

FOR TWO

Simple to make,
authentic Japanese dishes

Kurumi Hayter

APPLE

To my husband Simon,
for his support and encouragement.
And with special thanks to my mother Keiko.

A QUINTET BOOK
Published by The Apple Press
6 Blundell Street
London N7 9BH

ISBN 1-85076-668-1

This book was designed and produced by
Quintet Publishing Limited
6 Blundell Street
London N7 9BH

CREATIVE DIRECTOR: *Richard Dewing*
DESIGNER: *Simon Balley*
PROJECT EDITOR: *Diana Steedman*
EDITOR: *Deborah Taylor*
PHOTOGRAPHER: *David Armstrong*

Typeset in Great Britain by
Central Southern Typesetters, Eastbourne
Manufactured by Eray Scan Pte Ltd, Singapore
Printed by Star Standard Industries (Pte) Ltd, Singapore

The Publishers are grateful to Také Ltd,
Camden Town, London, to
Asuka Japanese Restaurant, Baker Street, London,
and to Mrs Yuko Hishitani for supplying
crockery for photography.

CONTENTS

PREFACE

The cuisine of south-east Asia has enjoyed a boom in popularity over the past few years and it is now common to find books on Thai and Indonesian cooking (to name but two) on the shelves of every high street book shop. So it is surprising that many people find themselves hard put to name any Japanese foods, with the exception of the most famous dishes like Tempura and Sushi, when asked what Japanese foods they are familiar with. People invariably think of Japanese cookery and its preparation as an esoteric art requiring years of training and experience to master. This misunderstanding is a great pity because Japanese cookery not only encompasses as great a range of flavours and textures as any other country in Asia but also, for the most part, is easily and quickly prepared.

This book aims to introduce a wide selection of delicious recipes that require no special skills or training to prepare. I sincerely hope that both the eating and making of the dishes in this book are a pleasurable and interesting experience.

INTRODUCTION

THE FLAVOURS OF JAPANESE COOKERY

The three basic flavours of cooking are saltiness, sweetness and sourness. These flavours are produced in Japanese cooking by the use, either singly or in combination, of the following 'building block' ingredients:

- soy sauce
- *miso* (a fermented soya bean paste)
- Japanese rice wine or *sake*
- *mirin* (a mixture of a variant of *sake* with sugar)
- *dashi* (a Japanese stock made from dried bonito or dried kelp or a mixture of the two depending on the flavour desired)
- sea salt
- caster sugar

BASIC TECHNIQUES

One of the great advantages to Japanese cookery is that to begin experimenting requires little investment in equipment over and above what is contained in the average Western kitchen. As for ingredients, the purchase of a bottle of Japanese soy sauce, *sake, mirin,* and some instant *dashi* granules (the latter two being widely available from health shops as well as Japanese or Chinese food shops) will enable any cook to prepare most of the recipes in this book.

Broadly speaking, there are three methods of preparation commonly used by the Japanese cook.

Grilling or *YAKI-MONO*

Grilling is the fastest cooking technique in the Japanese repertoire. Most commonly the meat, fish or vegetable prepared in this manner is first skewered before being grilled. In many cases, grilling takes place after the food has been steeped in a marinade. Sometimes it is brushed with a sauce or glaze while being grilled. A technique used when cooking fish involves the liberal sprinkling of salt onto the fish prior to grilling.

Simmering or *NI-MONO*

Ni-mono dishes commonly feature a mixture of either meat and vegetables or fish and vegetables and, less often, just fish or vegetables on their own. Some *ni-mono* require the use of a stock, whereas others depend only on the inclusion of soy sauce, *mirin* and occasionally sugar or *sake* to enhance their flavour.

Deep frying or *AGE-MONO*

Tempura, possibly the most widely known ambassador of Japanese cookery, is only one of a number of deep-fried dishes in the Japanese repertoire, which includes deep-fried vegetables, fish and meats. A number of different coatings are used in Japanese deep frying, including a plain flour batter in the case of *Tempura,* potato flour and breadcrumbs.

PREPARING MEAT

Very thinly sliced meat is common in Japanese cookery. An advantage of thin slicing is that it creates an impression of volume even with small amounts. Also, thin slices cook quickly. If you cannot find thinly sliced meat, ask your butcher to slice it or half freeze the cut of meat you purchase and then slice it yourself.

PREPARING VEGETABLES

There are three cutting styles used by Japanese cooks.

1 *Ran giri* or chopping at random. Peel, then roll around in your hand each time you chop, cutting to create asymmetrical shapes.

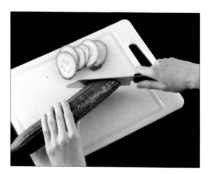

2 *Naname wa-giri* or slicing on a slant. Cut on a slant to create larger pieces.

3 *Sengiri* or slicing into matchsticks. Cut larger slices into matchstick-sized pieces.

THE ETIQUETTE OF EATING

Chopsticks are one of many Chinese inventions that have been assimilated into Japanese culture and are called *o-hashi*. Using chopsticks is no more difficult than using a knife and fork, as long as the user knows the correct way to hold them. Follow the directions illustrated below and you should have no problem eating with *o-hashi*.

❶ Think of your chopsticks as jaws that have been turned upside down. The lower chopstick, clamped between the tip of your ring finger, inner joint of your thumb and the knuckle of your index finger, remains fixed in the same position during eating.

❷ The upper chopstick is then held in the tips of your middle and index fingers and thumb so that it can be opened and closed in relation to the lower chopstick.

There are some basic principles of etiquette:

● Don't hold your chopsticks over a dish while deciding what to eat (*mayoi-bashi*).

● Don't spear food with your chopsticks (*sashi-bashi*).

● Don't use your chopsticks to pull a dish toward you or push it away from you (*yose-bashi*).

● Never pass food between chopsticks as this mirrors the Buddhist practice of handling the bones of the dead (*hashi-watashi*).

● Use your left hand to hold the rice bowl and your right hand to use your chopsticks. For left-handers, the reverse is correct.

● When in a formal situation do not eat food directly from a large, communal dish. Instead, first place food from the large dish into the small dish that is provided for your individual portion and then eat from that.

● Japanese noodles, or *men*, can be slurped with gusto while holding the noodles between your chopsticks. But Japanese soups or *sui-mono* should be sipped with more reserve.

PREPARING AND SERVING A JAPANESE MEAL

The Western concept of serving a dinner as a succession of courses is alien to traditional Japanese cookery. All the dishes in a Japanese meal are served to the diner as a set with the exception of dessert, which is not considered as an integral part of a Japanese meal, although fresh fruits are often provided at the end together with green tea. A true Japanese dinner always includes rice, a soup and a small dish of Japanese pickles, which are accompanied by a main dish of fish or meat together with a small side dish. A larger arrangement, for example a dinner party, would be achieved by adding a second side dish and perhaps a second main dish as well, depending on the occasion. A good host will attempt to vary each of the dishes so that the meal will combine as many different flavours, textures and types of preparation as possible. An example of this food-combining for a dinner party might be: grilled fish and deep fried chicken nuggets served as main dishes, braised soya beans and spinach sprinkled with sesame seeds and soy sauce as side dishes, and rice, a soup and a small serving of pickled vegetables as accompaniments. You may wonder how the cook manages to juggle so many dishes simultaneously and serve them all at once. The simple answer is that generally Japanese cooks make most of the dishes well in advance. Some dishes are re-heated prior to serving, others served only warm rather than hot. Exceptions to this include dishes cooked at the table such as *sukiyaki*, soups and noodles which should always be fresh and hot.

Japanese drinks

Today, the traditional Japanese rice liquor, *sake*, is a less frequent accompaniment to a Japanese dinner than it used to be. Many Japanese now choose lager-type beers to drink at their dinner table. The non-alcoholic alternative to these drinks is Japanese green tea or *o-cha*.

JAPANESE FISH STOCK

DASHI

D*ashi* or Japanese Fish Stock, is an essential
ingredient in Japanese cookery. It can be made from
katsuo-bushi (flaked bonito) or *konbu* (kelp). Some *dashi*
are a combination of the two variants and it is this stock
that is given here. There are two classes of *dashi*: 'premier',
which is used in Japanese consommé, *chawan mushi* and
miso soup, and normal *dashi* which is suitable for
simmered dishes and noodles or for use as a supplement to
premier *dashi*.

PREMIER DASHI	NORMAL DASHI
MAKES 800 ML (1½ PINTS) STOCK	**MAKES 1 LITRE (1¾ PINTS) STOCK**
1 litre (1¼ pints) water	*1.2 litres (2 pints) water*
15 cm (6 in) strip dried konbu *or kelp, cut into three pieces*	*dried* konbu *and bonito flakes from making* Premier dashi
30 g (1 oz) dried bonito *flakes*	*15 g (½ oz) dried* bonito *flakes*

❶ Put the water and *konbu* in a pan and slowly bring to the boil over a medium heat. Just before the liquid reaches boiling point, remove the *konbu* and add the *bonito* flakes. When the flakes begin to rise and the liquid bubbles, turn off the heat. Wait until the flakes have sunk to the bottom of the pan.

❶ Put the water, used *konbu* and *bonito* flakes, and the dried *bonito* flakes in a pan together. Bring to the boil and simmer over a medium heat until the liquid has reduced by about a third. Strain through muslin or a large coffee filter.

❷ The *konbu* and *bonito* flakes can be retained to make normal *dashi* at another time.

DASHI STOCK GRANULES

Instant dashi can be made from freeze-dried stock granules, which is a convenient, no fuss alternative although opinions differ as to whether the taste of instant dashi is a match for the 'real thing' or not. If you buy instant dashi and the instructions turn out to be in Japanese use the following instructions.

In a pan, stir 1 heaped teaspoon of granules into 600 ml (1 pint) of cold water and bring to the boil.

MISO SOUP with Wakame Seaweed and Onion

WAKAME TO TAMA-NEGI NO MISO-SHIRU

M*iso shiru* is the easiest soup you will ever make. In Japan, it is served at breakfast, lunch or dinner, when it is accompanied by a main dish and a bowl of rice.

Wakame seaweed and *tofu* are the two most common ingredients used in the soup and are either used alone or are complemented by fresh, chopped vegetables. *Miso* soup varies according to the tastes of every family and each household has its own favourite combinations.

Unlike Western soups, Japanese soup is sipped from the bowl with any pieces of vegetable or *tofu* being eaten with chopsticks.

INGREDIENTS

500 ml (18 fl oz) dashi *stock* (*see p. 13*)
½ *medium onion, sliced*
2 *teaspoons dried* wakame *seaweed*
2 *tablespoons* miso *paste*

1 Put the *dashi* stock and onion in a pan, bring to the boil and simmer until the onion becomes transparent.

2 Add the *wakame* and continue to simmer until it has expanded. (This only takes a couple of minutes.)

3 Add the *miso* paste and stir using a small whisk, until dissolved. Heat for a few more minutes until the soup starts to boil. Do not boil for more than 1–2 minutes or the soup will be too salty. Serve immediately.

14

MISO SOUP with Silken *Tofu* and Spring Onions

KINU DOFU TO NEGI NO MISO-SHIRU

Two types of *tofu* are widely used in Japanese cookery, *kinu* or silken *tofu* and *momen* or cotton *tofu*. As the names suggest, *kinu dofu* has a very smooth, silky texture whereas *momen dofu* is characterised by its more solid, coarser appearance and feel. It is *kinu dofu* that is usually used in *miso* soups.

INGREDIENTS

500 ml (18 fl oz) dashi stock (see p. 13)
100 g (4 oz) silken tofu, cut into 1 cm (½ in) cubes
3 spring onions, chopped
2 tablespoons miso paste

❶ Put the *dashi* stock and *tofu* in a pan, bring to the boil and simmer for 4–5 minutes.

❷ Add the spring onions and simmer for a further minute. Stir the *miso* paste into the soup using a mini whisk until it is completely dissolved. Simmer again until the soup just returns to the boil. Serve immediately.

EGG AND LEEK Consommé

TAMAGO NO SUMASHI JIRU

This clear soup is usually eaten with *sushi* dishes and has a subtle flavour. The use of shiitake mushrooms adds extra taste. Do not boil the leek for too long as it needs to retain some of its texture.

INGREDIENTS

500 ml (18 fl oz) dashi stock (see p. 13)

2.5 cm (1 in) leek, halved and sliced very finely

3 shiitake mushrooms, sliced

½ teaspoon salt

A dash of soy sauce

1 egg, beaten

❶ In a pan bring the *dashi* stock to the boil then add the leek, mushrooms, salt and soy sauce. Simmer for 3–4 minutes.

❷ Gradually add the beaten egg to the pan, whisking continuously to stop it from forming into lumps. Serve immediately.

SIMMERED BEEF and Potatoes

GYUNIKU NO NIKU-JAGA

This dish is one of several described in Japan as "mother's taste dishes" and it is very much a family-style creation.

INGREDIENTS

40 ml (1½ fl oz) *water*

1½ tablespoons sake

2 tablespoons *caster sugar*

2 tablespoons *soy sauce*

225 g (8 oz) *thinly sliced beef, cut into 5 cm (2 in) lengths*

255 g (9 oz) *potatoes, peeled and cut into bite-sized pieces*

85 g (3 oz) *frozen peas*

1 Put the water, *sake*, sugar and soy sauce in a pan and bring to the boil.

2 Add the meat and simmer for a few minutes or until the meat browns. Remove from the pan and set aside. Put the potatoes in the pan and simmer, covered, for 10 minutes or until tender. Add the peas and simmer for a further 3 minutes.

3 Return the meat back to the pan and simmer for about 3 minutes. Serve hot with a bowl of rice and one or two vegetable dishes.

HAMBURGERS with Shiitake Mushroom Sauce

BEEF HAMBURGER NO SHIITAKE SAUSU

This is a contemporary combination of Western substance with Japanese form. The sauce retains the delicate flavour of the shiitake mushrooms partnered by the punchy flavours of the ginger and soy sauce.

INGREDIENTS	FOR THE SHIITAKE SAUCE
25 ml (1 fl oz) vegetable oil	50 g (2 oz) shiitake mushrooms, sliced
1 small onion, finely chopped	150 ml (5 fl oz) water
½ sliced brown loaf made into breadcrumbs	1 tablespoon sake
1½ tablespoons milk	1 tablespoon soy sauce
225 g (8 oz) minced beef	½ in piece root ginger, peeled
½ teaspoon salt	2 teaspoons cornflour
Freshly ground black pepper	
½ egg, beaten	

❶ Heat 2 teaspoons of oil in a frying pan and fry the onion until golden brown. Soak the breadcrumbs in milk for 5 minutes. Grate the ginger and squeeze to extract the juices.

❷ Place the beef, onion, seasoning and egg in a bowl and mix thoroughly.

❸ Divide the mixture into two. Moisten your hands with water, then shape into burgers.

❹ Heat the remaining oil in the frying pan and fry the hamburgers for about 5 minutes on each side or until cooked. Remove and set aside.

❺ Add the shiitake mushrooms to the frying pan then add the water, sake, soy sauce, ginger juice. Season with salt and pepper. Bring to the boil and cook for 1 minute before adding the cornflour diluted in a small amount of water, to thicken. Pour over the burgers and serve.

STEAK with Garlic and Soy Sauce

STEAK NO NIN-NIKU SAUSU

A combination of a Western cut of meat with a Japanese sauce that works really well. Remember that the frying times given for the steak will vary depending on the thickness of the meat and personal preference. This flexible dish can be served with Japanese side dishes or a Western accompaniment of vegetables.

INGREDIENTS

2 x 150–200 g (5–7 oz) sirloin or rump steaks
Freshly ground black pepper
1 tablespoon vegetable oil
5 garlic cloves, sliced
1 tablespoon sake
15 g (½ oz) butter
1 tablespoon soy sauce

1 Beat the meat on both sides using a steak hammer or a rolling pin, then season with the pepper.

2 Heat the oil in a frying pan and fry the garlic briefly. Remove and set aside.

3 Fry the steaks lightly on both sides, then add the *sake* and fry for a further minute before placing the steaks on warmed serving plates.

4 Return the garlic to the pan, add the butter and soy sauce and when the mixture begins to bubble pour over the steaks and serve immediately.

SUGGESTED FRYING TIMES
(For 150–200 g (5–7 oz) steak)

Rare: 3 minutes on each side
Medium-rare: 4 minutes on each side Well-done: 6 minutes on each side

STIR-FRIED PORK in Ginger with Onion

BUTA-NIKU NO SHOUGA YAKI

The sweet, tangy flavours of the soy sauce and ginger marinade are enriched and enhanced by the pork. Like most other Japanese dishes, *Buta-niku no shouga yaki* is easy to prepare and can be made in no time at all.

INGREDIENTS

225 g (8 oz) thinly sliced pork, cut into 5 cm (2 in) lengths

1 tablespoon vegetable oil

1 medium sized onion, peeled and sliced

FOR THE MARINADE

25 g (1 oz) root ginger, peeled, grated and squeezed

1½ tablespoons soy sauce

1 tablespoon sake

1 To make the marinade, mix together the juice of the ginger, the soy sauce and the *sake* in a bowl.

2 Add the pork and marinate for 30 minutes. Heat the oil in a frying pan and fry the onion until it is transparent. Remove and set aside.

3 Add the meat to the frying pan and fry for 5 minutes or until cooked.

4 Return the onion to the frying pan and stir-fry for a further 1–2 minutes.

5 Add the remaining marinade and stir-fry again for 1–2 minutes. Serve with a bowl of hot, plain boiled rice.

SIMMERED BELLY of Pork and Mouli

DAIKON TO BARA-NIKU NO UMA-NI

S immering is a widely used technique in Japanese cooking as it brings out the flavours of the ingredients. Its European equivalent, the mouli, contains more water than the Japanese giant radish or *daikon*, making it easier to cook. Taste-wise though, there is little difference between the two.

INGREDIENTS

2 teaspoons vegetable oil

225 g (8 oz) belly of pork, cut into
1 cm (½ in) lengths

225 g (8 oz) mouli, peeled and chopped
into randomly-shaped, bite-sized pieces

3 tablespoons sake

2 tablespoons soy sauce

1 Heat the oil in a saucepan and add the meat. Fry until browned.

2 Add the mouli and stir well, then add the *sake* and simmer, covered, for 10 minutes.

3 Add the soy sauce and continue to cook, covered for a further 5 minutes or until the mouli is cooked through. Serve hot with a bowl of boiled rice.

DEEP-FRIED PORK Steak in Breadcrumbs

TONKATSU

This is one of the most popular dishes in modern Japanese cuisine. It is usually served with shredded cabbage and garnished with tomato ketchup, brown sauce and/or mustard.

INGREDIENTS

2 x 150–200 g (5–7 oz) boneless pork loin steaks
2 tablespoons plain flour
1 egg, beaten
2–3 tablespoons dry white breadcrumbs
Vegetable oil, for deep frying

1 Beat the meat gently with a steak hammer or rolling pin to tenderize it. Dust with the flour then dip into the beaten egg.

2 Coat the steaks with the breadcrumbs.

3 Heat the oil to 170°C/330°F and then deep fry the steaks until cooked through, about 6 minutes, depending on the thickness of the steaks. Serve garnished with lettuce, sliced tomato and cucumber, adding tomato ketchup, brown sauce and mustard if you wish.

PORK MEATBALLS in Sweet Soy Sauce

NIKU-DANGO NO AMAKARA-NI

The use of minced meat is widespread in Japan and this form, *niku-dango*, is sold ready-made in delicatessens as well as being prepared at home. Take care, as the sweet-tasting sauce makes it all too easy to gorge oneself on these little balls of pork!

MAKES 16 MEATBALLS

FOR THE MEATBALLS

225 g (8 oz) minced pork
25 g (1 oz) leek, finely chopped
1 tablespoon sake
A large pinch of salt
½ egg, beaten
1 tablespoon cornflour
Vegetable oil, for deep frying

FOR THE SAUCE

4 tablespoons water
1 tablespoon sake
1 tablespoon mirin
1 tablespoon caster sugar
1 tablespoon soy sauce
2 teaspoons cornflour

1 To make the meatballs, mix the pork, leek, *sake*, salt, beaten egg and cornflour in a bowl. Knead the mixture until the beaten egg is well combined and gives a stickiness to the rest of the mixture. Then, take one tablespoon of the mixture in your hand and mould it into a ball.

2 Fill a pan about one-third full with cooking oil. Heat to 180°C/350°F and then deep fry the meatballs for 5 minutes or until browned. Remove and drain off any excess oil using absorbent kitchen paper.

3 Put the water, *sake*, *mirin*, caster sugar, soy sauce and cornflour together in a pan. Mix together over a low heat stirring until the sauce has thickened. Add the meatballs and continue to stir until they are all covered in the sauce. Serve with a bowl of hot, plain boiled rice and a vegetable dish.

JAPANESE CHICKEN Shish Kebab

YAKITORI

Yakitori lends its name to the Japanese *yakitori* bar, a popular place to meet, eat, drink and socialize throughout Japan. Chicken and chicken livers are the two most commonly eaten *yakitori*. They can be eaten with a sweet, soy sauce-based sauce or *tare*, as in the recipe below, or sprinkled liberally with salt or powdered chilli.

INGREDIENTS

FOR THE SAUCE	FOR THE YAKITORI
50 ml (2 fl oz) soy sauce	2 boneless chicken breasts (with skin) diced, making 24 pieces
50 ml (2 fl oz) mirin	
1 tablespoon caster sugar	1 leek, cut into 2.5 cm (1 in) lengths, making 8 pieces
1 tablespoon honey	
Skin from the chicken	½ green pepper, seeded and diced, making 8 pieces
	8 bamboo or steel skewers

1 To make the sauce, put the soy sauce, *mirin*, sugar, honey and chicken skin into a saucepan, bring to the boil and simmer for about 10 minutes or until thickened.

2 To prepare the *yakitori*, thread onto a skewer pieces of chicken, leek, chicken, green pepper and chicken again, in that order.

3 Pre-heat the grill to low and cook the *yakitori* until the meat has turned white (about 3 minutes).

4 Turn up the heat to medium and brush the *yakitori* with the sauce frequently, turning from time to time, for about 6–7 minutes or until the meat is cooked through. Serve with rice and a vegetable dish.

CHICKEN LIVERS with Peppers in a Sweet Soy Sauce

REBA TO PIMAN NO AMAKARA-NI

Chicken livers are widely eaten in Japan. Cooking in soy sauce and sugar disguises the smell of the liver, which some people find off-putting, and softens the flesh.

INGREDIENTS

280 g (10 oz) chicken livers, cut into bite-sized pieces
1 tablespoon vegetable oil
½ green pepper, seeded and thinly sliced lengthways
1½ tablespoons soy sauce
1½ tablespoons mirin
½ tablespoon caster sugar

1 Dip the livers into a bowl of boiling water until blanched, then drain.

2 Heat the oil in a frying pan and fry the green pepper for about 3 minutes. Remove and set aside.

3 Add the livers to the pan, frying over a medium heat for about 7 minutes. Sprinkle over the soy sauce, mirin and sugar and continue to cook, stirring, for about 5 minutes.

4 Return the green pepper to the pan and stir in lightly for a few minutes. Serve hot with rice and a vegetable dish.

DEEP-FRIED CHICKEN Nuggets

TORI NO KARA-AGE

The mixture of garlic, ginger and soy sauce enhances the taste of the chicken, with the sliced lemon giving refreshing 'bite' to these delicious nuggets.

INGREDIENTS

2 boneless chicken breasts, cut into bite-sized cubes

FOR THE MARINADE

3 tablespoons soy sauce

30 g (1 oz) root ginger, peeled and grated

2 large garlic cloves, peeled and grated

Salt and freshly ground black pepper

FOR THE COATING

2 tablespoons cornflour

2 tablespoons plain flour

Vegetable oil, for deep frying

2 slices lemon, to garnish

1 Marinate the chicken with the soy sauce, ginger, garlic, salt and pepper for 30 minutes.

2 Mix the cornflour with the plain flour. Take each piece of chicken from the marinade and roll in the flour mixture until completely coated.

3 Heat the oil to 180°C/350°F and deep-fry the chicken pieces for 4–5 minutes or until a burnished golden brown. Garnish with the sliced lemon and serve on a bed of salad leaves.

TOFU HAMBURGER

TOFU HAMBURGER

A modern, healthy Japanese variation of an American favourite. The *tofu* should be *momen* (coarser, solid *tofu*) which needs to be left to drain for a few minutes before it is used so that it is not too watery.

MAKES 4 BURGERS

25 g (1 oz) carrot, chopped
2 spring onions, chopped
140 g (5 oz) minced chicken
200 g (7 oz) momen, or "cotton" tofu
½ egg, beaten
1 tablespoon fresh breadcrumbs
1 tablespoon plain flour
Salt and freshly ground black pepper
1 tablespoon vegetable oil
2 slices lemon, to garnish
Soy sauce, to serve

1 Mince the carrot and spring onion in a food processor. Add the chicken, tofu, egg, breadcrumbs, flour, salt and pepper and continue to process until well mixed.

2 Divide the mixture into 4 equal portions and form into burger shapes.

3 Heat the oil in a pan and fry the burgers over a low heat for about 8 minutes each side or until browned. Serve with the soy sauce and garnish with the lemon slices.

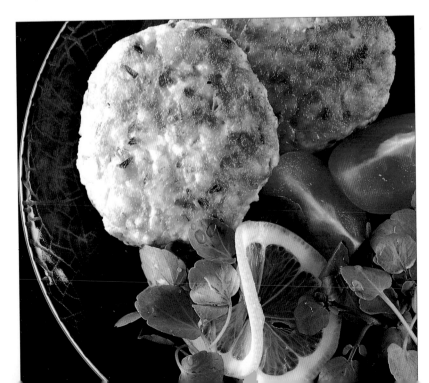

FRIED MARINATED Herrings

NISHIN NO TSUKE-YAKI

This is an easy-to-prepare and quick meal. Marinating the herrings in *sake* and soy sauce adds extra flavour.

INGREDIENTS

2 large or 4 small herrings, gutted and boned

2 tablespoons plain flour

2 tablespoons vegetable oil

FOR THE MARINADE	FOR THE DRESSING
4 teaspoons sake	4 teaspoons soy sauce
4 teaspoons soy sauce	2 teaspoons wine vinegar
	1 teaspoon caster sugar

1 Mix together the *sake* and soy sauce, then pour over the herrings and marinate for 30 minutes, turning 2 or 3 times.

2 Meanwhile, make the dressing by mixing the soy sauce, vinegar and sugar in a bowl.

3 Wipe the herrings with absorbent kitchen paper and then coat with the flour.

4 Heat the vegetable oil in a frying pan and fry the herrings for about 3 minutes on each side or until the flour coating is golden brown. Serve with rice and a vegetable dish.

DEEP-FRIED MACKEREL

SABA NO TASUTA-AGE

The venerable mackerel is one of the mainstays of the Japanese diet and can be prepared in numerous ways. *Age-mono*, or deep-frying, locks in the mackerel's oils and this gives its flesh a meat-like quality.

INGREDIENTS

1 x 450 g (1 lb) mackerel, head removed and gutted
1 tablespoon soy sauce
½ tablespoon sake
½ fresh chilli, seeded and finely chopped
1 cm (½ in) cube root ginger, crushed
2–3 tablespoons cornflour
Vegetable oil, for deep frying

1 Cut the mackerel in half slicing close to one side of the back bone. Repeat the same process on the other side. Now you have 2 fillets separated from the back bone. Remove as many bones from the fillets as possible without spoiling the flesh (a pair of tweezers is helpful). Cut each fillet into three pieces.

2 Put the soy sauce, *sake*, chilli and ginger into a dish and marinate the fish for 20 minutes.

3 Dry the fish using absorbent kitchen paper to remove any excess moisture, then coat in the cornflour. Heat the oil to 180°C/350°F then deep fry the fish for about 4 minutes. Serve with stir-fried vegetables and sprinkle with soy sauce.

GRILLED SALTED TROUT

MASU NO SHIO-YAKI

Grilling is a very simple way of cooking fish. The trout need to be fresh to make the most of this dish.

INGREDIENTS

2 medium trout, gutted

1 teaspoon salt

Soy sauce, to serve

1 Make 3 cuts on each side of the fish, place them on a wire tray and sprinkle both sides with salt.

2 Grill for 5–6 minutes or until lightly browned, then turn and grill for a further 5–6 minutes. (Remember the grilling time will vary depending on the size of the fish). When the fish is ready, transfer to a plate and drizzle with soy sauce. Serve with rice and a vegetable dish.

SIMMERED MACKEREL in Miso Sauce

SABA NO MISO-NI

This dish is a particular favourite in autumn, when the *saba* (mackerel) is reputed to be at its best. The *saba* is cooked unboned to give extra flavour.

INGREDIENTS

1 x 450 g (1 lb) mackerel, head removed and gutted

FOR THE SAUCE

100 ml (4 fl oz) water

2 tablespoons caster sugar

1 tablespoon sake

50 g (2 oz) miso

1 thin slice peeled root ginger

2 spring onions, cut in half

1 Cut the mackerel in half close to one side of the back bone to make 2 pieces of fish, one with the back bone attached and one without. Cut each piece in half again.

2 Put the water, sugar, sake and miso in a pan then heat until the liquid is simmering. Add the fish and ginger and continue to simmer, covered, for 7–8 minutes with a lid, slightly smaller than the pan and placed directly onto the fish. Use aluminium foil if you do not have a lid.

3 Add the spring onions and simmer for a further 5–10 minutes. Serve immediately with rice and a vegetable dish.

SIMMERED SQUID with Mouli

DAIKON TO IKA NO UMA-NI

The flavour of this dish comes from the subtle taste of the squid combined with the fresh mouli. Mouli, the Italian giant radish, is easier to cook than Japanese daikon, because of its higher water content.

INGREDIENTS

1 x 300 g (10 oz) squid
300 g (10 oz) mouli, peeled, cut in half lengthways and cut into 1 cm (½ in) widths
50 ml (2 fl oz) sake
40 ml (1½ oz) soy sauce
100 ml (4 fl oz) water

1 Pull the head and tentacles from the squid, then remove the transparent centre bone and wash the body cavity. Take off the skin, then cut the head from the tentacles.

2 Cut the body and legs of the squid into 1 cm (½ in) widths and blanch in boiling water. Put the mouli in a pan and cover with cold water. Bring to the boil and simmer for about 6 minutes until the mouli has become almost transparent, then drain.

3 Heat the *sake* in a pan with the soy sauce. When it boils, add the squid and simmer for about 4 minutes. Remove the squid with a slotted spoon and set aside.

4 Add the water and drained mouli to the pan, simmer, covered, for about 7 minutes. Put the squid in the pan with the mouli and simmer for 3–4 minutes. Serve with rice and a vegetable dish.

魚

FRIED AUBERGINE and Green Pepper in Sweet Miso Sauce

NASU NO NABE-SHIGI

Autumn is the season for aubergines in Japan, when greengrocers stock their shelves with the numerous varieties available. Japanese aubergines vary greatly in length though none possess the girth of those typically produced in Europe or the United States.

INGREDIENTS

2 tablespoons sesame oil

1 medium onion, peeled and cut into bite-sized pieces

1 x 200 g (8 oz) aubergine cut into bite-sized pieces and soaked in water

½ green pepper, cut into bite-sized pieces

FOR THE SWEET MISO SAUCE

40 g (1½ oz) miso paste

2 tablespoons caster sugar

2 tablespoons water

2 tablespoons mirin

1 Heat 1 tablespoon of sesame oil in a pan and fry the onion for 3–4 minutes. Add the rest of the oil and the aubergine and continue to fry for 3–4 minutes. Add the green pepper and fry until the aubergine has softened.

2 Mix together the *miso* paste, sugar, water and *mirin* in a bowl, then add to the pan, stirring for 1–2 minutes. Serve hot as a side dish.

SPINACH with *Bonito* Flakes and Soy Sauce

HOURENSO NO O-HITASHI

F resh spinach is vital to make this delicious, nutritious dish. Take care not to overcook the spinach or you will destroy its vitamins.

INGREDIENTS

225 g (8 oz) spinach leaves, rinsed and drained
A pinch of salt
A large pinch of bonito fish flakes
2–3 tablespoons soy sauce

1 Boil the spinach in salted water for about 2 minutes or until lightly cooked.

2 Drain and quickly rinse with cold water to cool and avoid discolouration.

3 Holding the leaves in a bunch at the stem, squeeze out any excess water.

4 Cut the bunch into 2.5 cm (1 in) lengths. Place in a small bowl or dish and sprinkle with the bonito flakes, followed by a drizzle of soy sauce. Serve as a side dish.

BRAISED SWEET POTATOES

SATSUMA-IMO NO AMA-NI

Atraditional favourite, sweet potatoes are eaten throughout the year in Japan. This simple dish brings out their delicate sweetness.

INGREDIENTS

350 g (12 oz) sweet potatoes, cut into
1 cm (½ in) pieces

200 ml (7 fl oz) water

A pinch of salt

1 tablespoon caster sugar

1 teaspoon soy sauce

1 With a knife, bevel off the edges of the sweet potato. This will help prevent them breaking up while they are cooking.

2 Put the potatoes, water, salt, caster sugar and soy sauce into a large pan, making sure that the pieces of potato are laid flat on the bottom. Bring to the boil, then simmer, covered, for 10–15 minutes, until the potatoes have softened, removing the lid for the last 5 minutes. (Remember that the simmering time required will depend on the type of sweet potatoes you use.) Serve as a side dish.

SIMMERED CABBAGE and Bacon

CABETSU TO BECON NO NI-BITASHI

Japanese cabbage has a softer texture than those available in Britain. Accordingly, I think it is best to discard, or use for another recipe, the tougher, outer leaves of the cabbage and use only the inner leaves for this dish. Because of its distinctive taste Savoy cabbage is best avoided. Try not to overcook the cabbage or it will become limp. The leaves should be cooked but still have some crunch left in them.

INGREDIENTS

185 g (6.5 oz) cabbage leaves, cut into
2.5 cm (1 in) squares

2 rashers of unsmoked bacon, cut into
2.5 cm (1 in) lengths

250 ml (9 fl oz) dashi stock (see p. 13)

2 teaspoons soy sauce

2 teaspoons vegetable oil

1 Heat the oil in a pan and fry the bacon over a low heat until cooked.

2 Add the cabbage and fry, stirring, for 2 minutes.

3 Add the *dashi* stock and soy sauce. Simmer, covered for 10 minutes, or until the cabbage has softened. Stir occasionally. Serve as a side dish.

STIR-FRIED MANGETOUT and Corned Beef

SAYA-INGEN TO CORNBEEF NO ITAME-MONO

It has been said many times that the Japanese are a nation of innovators and this dish illustrates the Japanese habit of absorbing a foreign influence into their culture and then enhancing it with a distinctive Japanese flavour. The mangetout should be firm so be careful not to overcook them.

INGREDIENTS

150 g (5 oz) mangetout, rinsed and trimmed
1 tablespoon vegetable oil
100 g (4 oz) corned beef, chopped
1 teaspoon soy sauce
Salt and freshly ground black pepper

1 Boil the mangetout in salted, boiling water for 3 minutes, then drain.

2 Heat the oil in a frying pan. Add the corned beef and stir-fry for 5 minutes over a medium heat.

3 Add the mangetout, sprinkle with salt and pepper and stir-fry for another 5 minutes. Sprinkle with the soy sauce. Serve hot as a side dish.

CHINESE LEAVES and Cockles in Mustard and Soy Sauce

HAKUSAI TO TORI-GAI NO KARASHI-JOYU AE

Cockles are not very common in Japan, and clams are usually used for this dish. But cockles go so well with the other ingredients, they make an excellent and economical substitute. You can use fresh cockles or those sold in jars or tins.

INGREDIENTS

150 g (5 oz) Chinese leaves

4 spring onions

½ tablespoon soy sauce

1 teaspoon English mustard

1 teaspoon mirin

90 g (3½ oz) cockles, drained

❶ Bring a saucepan of water to the boil, add the Chinese leaves and cook for 3 minutes. Then, add the spring onions and boil for a further 2 minutes. Drain and rinse lightly with cold water, then squeeze out any excess water. Cut into 2.5 cm (1 in) lengths.

❷ Mix the soy sauce, mustard and mirin in a large bowl. Add the Chinese leaves, spring onion and cockles and mix. Serve as a side dish or as a starter.

GREEN BEANS in a Sesame Dressing

INGEN NO GOMA-AE

Sesame enjoys a reputation of being a healthy food in Japan and both black and white sesame are common ingredients in Japanese cuisine. To toast the seeds for this recipe, simply put them in a frying pan without oil then heat while stirring until the seeds have puffed up and you can smell the distinctive aroma of sesame.

INGREDIENTS

175 g (6 oz) frozen whole green beans

A pinch of salt

FOR THE DRESSING

1 tablespoon toasted sesame seeds

1 tablespoon caster sugar

¾ tablespoon dashi stock (see p. 13)

½ tablespoon miso paste

1 tablespoon soy sauce

1 Boil the beans in a pan of boiling water for 5 minutes or until tender.

2 Finely grind the sesame seeds in a pestle and mortar or in a coffee grinder. Add the sugar, *dashi, miso* paste and soy sauce and mix together well.

3 Toss the green beans in the sesame dressing and serve as a side dish.

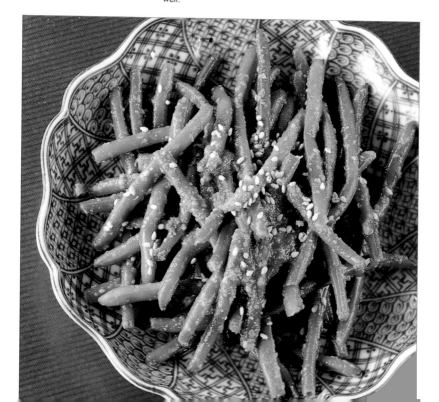

SIMMERED Mixed Vegetables

YASAI NO NI-MONO

The potato is not a staple part of the Japanese diet but is nevertheless much used in Japanese cookery. It is usually diced and cooked with other vegetables as in this dish.

INGREDIENTS

200 ml (7 fl oz) dashi stock (see p. 13)

100 g (4 oz) carrots, peeled and chopped at random into bite-sized pieces

225 g (8 oz) potatoes, peeled and cut into bite-sized pieces

1 medium onion, sliced

2 teaspoons caster sugar

½ tablespoon mirin

A pinch of salt

1 tablespoon soy sauce

50 g (2 oz) frozen, whole green beans, halved

❶ Put the *dashi*, carrots and potatoes in a pan. Bring to the boil and simmer, covered, for 5 minutes.

❷ Add the onion, sugar, *mirin*, salt and soy sauce and continue to simmer, covered, for a further 5 minutes.

❸ Finally, add the beans and simmer as before for 4 minutes. Serve hot as a side dish.

SEAFOOD SALAD with *Ponzu Dressing*

KANI KAMOBOKO IRI SALADA

Ponzu can be used as a dip sauce (see Cod and Chinese Cabbage Pot on page 72) or as a tangy, non-oily salad dressing. It is equally good used in both ways.

INGREDIENTS

2 celery sticks
7.5 cm (3 in) piece cucumber
90 g (3½ oz) carrot, peeled
50 g (2 oz) frozen whole green beans
5 seafood sticks
A pinch of salt
1 quantity of ponzu dressing (see p. 72)

1 Slice the celery, cucumber and carrot on a slant then cut into matchsticks (see p.9 for more information).

2 Cook the green beans in salted boiling water for 4–5 minutes, then rinse with cold water, drain and cut in half.

3 Mix the vegetables together on a plate or in a bowl. Then pull the seafood sticks into strands with your fingers and use to garnish the top of the salad. Drizzle with the *ponzu* dressing on serving.

野菜

TEMPURA

TEMPURA

 One of the most famous dishes in the Japanese
repertoire, *Tempura* needs no introduction. Ironically,
strong evidence exists that *Tempura* is not originally
Japanese, but was introduced into Japan by Portuguese
traders in the seventeenth century. One of the great
advantages of *Tempura* is its versatility. Virtually any
seafood and vegetable can be prepared and served in this
way. The ingredients suggested below are those most
commonly served in Japan. Mix the dip first, so that the
Tempura can be served and eaten immediately after being
fried.

INGREDIENTS

*½ green pepper, seeded and cut into
four pieces lengthwise*

4 shiitake mushrooms

*½ lb sweet potatoes, unpeeled but
sliced into ¼ in circles*

*¼ lb carrots, peeled and cut into 2½ in lengths,
then cut into matchsticks*

4 large shrimp, peeled but tails on

Vegetable oil, for deep frying

A little all-purpose flour

1 small mouli, peeled and grated

FOR THE BATTER

¾ cup all-purpose flour

¼ cup cornstarch

1 egg, beaten

¾ cup water

FOR THE DIP

2 tablespoons mirin

2 tablespoons soy sauce

¼ cup dashi stock (see p.13)

1 To make the dip, put the
mirin, soy sauce, and *dashi*
stock in a pan, bring to a boil,
and simmer for 1 minute. Leave
to cool.

2 To make the batter, place the
flour, cornstarch, egg, and
water into a bowl and mix
lightly using chopsticks or a
fork. The batter should be quite
lumpy with some flour visible on
top of the mixture.

3 Heat the oil in a pan to
350°F. Check the temperature
by dropping in some batter or
a piece of bread; if it bubbles
and floats to the surface, the oil
is at the right temperature.

5 Dip the vegetables into the batter and deep-fry until the batter has turned golden brown. Check the harder vegetables, such as sweet potatoes, are cooked by piercing with a skewer. If it runs through smoothly with no resistance, the vegetables are ready. The carrot matchsticks should be picked up in small bunches, dipped in the batter and then fried, held together by the batter.

6 To deep-fry the shrimp, coat them with a little flour before dipping into the batter as this will stop them from spitting while frying. When all the ingredients have been fried, serve immediately. Place the dip in small bowls and into the center, add a spoonful of grated mouli. Dip the pieces of *Tempura* into the dip before eating. The dip and grated mouli should be replenished throughout the meal.

JAPANESE-STYLE OMELETTE

TAMAGO-YAKI

O ften served for breakfast in Japan, *tamago-yaki* requires a little more skill and patience than a Western omelette, but the delicious result is well worth the extra effort. It is essential to use a non-stick frying pan to get a really good result.

INGREDIENTS

2 eggs
½ tablespoon caster sugar
½ tablespoon soy sauce
½ tablespoon dashi *stock (see p.13)*
A pinch of salt
Vegetable oil, for frying

1 Break the eggs into a bowl, add the sugar, soy sauce, *dashi* stock and salt and mix well. Heat the oil in a non-stick frying pan over a low heat. Pour one quarter of the egg mixture into the frying pan.

2 Just before the surface of the egg starts to get firm, carefully flip over the edge and roll up. Store on one side of the pan.

3 Holding up the rolled omelette with a fish slice or chopstick, add a second quarter of the egg mixture, making sure that it spreads beneath the already cooked roll.

4 Again, just before the egg begins to firm, roll around the completed roll and store on the other side of the pan. Repeat this process with the two remaining quarters of egg mixture. Cool before cutting into 2.5 cm (1 in) lengths. When served as a side dish, sprinkle with soy sauce.

SEAWEED-WRAPPED Avocado

AVOCADO TO NORI

Avocado is not a traditional ingredient of Japanese cooking but it is certainly popular in many Japanese homes. This popularity is said to be due to the similarity between the taste of the avocado and the taste of raw tuna as used in *sushi* and *sashimi*. You can mix in *wasabi*, the green Japanese mustard powder, to spice up the soy sauce, which can be used as a dressing, if you wish.

INGREDIENTS

1 avocado
Nori (*2 sheets of dried seaweed*)
2 teaspoons soy sauce
1 teaspoon wasabi (*optional*)

1 Slice the avocado in two, remove the stone and peel. Cut in half again, then slice into 1 cm (½ in) widths.

2 Cut the nori into strips and wrap the avocado slices in the *nori*.

3 Pour soy sauce into a small dish. If you are using *wasabi*, mash in a small amount. Dip the avocado into the sauce before eating.

SALTED CABBAGE and Cucumber

CABETSU TO KYUURI NO SHIO-MOMI

This quickly-prepared side dish makes a superb partner to fresh cooked white rice. A sharp knife will help you with the cucumber.

INGREDIENTS

100 g (4 oz) green cabbage (preferably the softer, inner leaves)

4 cm (1½ in) cucumber, halved lengthways

1 teaspoon salt

1 small red chilli, seeded and finely chopped

❶ Cut the stalks out of the cabbage leaves, then slice the leaves lengthways, before cutting into 1 cm (½ in) widths. Slice the two halves of the cucumber as finely as you can.

❷ Put the cabbage and cucumber in a bowl and sprinkle with the salt. Leave for 30 minutes, then squeeze out any excess liquid from the vegetables with your hands.

❸ Add the chilli and mix well. Leave for 5 minutes.

❹ Sprinkle with soy sauce just before serving.

SALTED TURNIP with Lemon

KABU NO SOKUSEKI-ZUKE

This dish is one of many Japanese *tsukemono* or pickles. The freshness of the turnip is essential for success.

INGREDIENTS

2 x 100 g (4 oz) turnips peeled, halved
and thinly sliced

1 teaspoon salt

3 lemon slices, cut into quarters

1 teaspoon soy sauce

1 Place the sliced turnip in a bowl, sprinkle with the salt and leave for 20–30 minutes.

2 Rub the turnip until it is soft, then squeeze out any excess liquid.

3 Add the lemon quarters, then drizzle with soy sauce. Serve as a side dish.

SIMMERED *HIJIKI* SEAWEED

HIJIKI NO NI-MONO

H*ijiki* is one of the many types of seaweed used in Japanese cookery. *Hijiki* is a very healthy source of several minerals including calcium and iodine and vitamin B^{12}.

INGREDIENTS

20 g (¼ oz) *dried* hijiki
½ *sheet* abura-age
50 g (2 oz) *carrots, peeled, and cut into short matchsticks*
2 *teaspoons vegetable oil*
250 ml (8 fl oz) dashi stock (*see p. 13*)
1½ *tablespoons caster sugar*
1½ *tablespoons soy sauce*
1 *tablespoon* mirin

1 Rinse the *hijiki* then soak in a bowlful of water for 20–30 minutes. Rinse then drain again. The *hijiki* should swell to six or seven times its original size.

2 Rinse the *abura-age* with hot water, then cut into small slices, about the same size as the carrot.

3 Heat the oil in a saucepan and fry the *hijiki, abura-age* and carrots for 1 minute.

4 Add the *dashi* stock, sugar, soy sauce and *mirin*, then simmer, uncovered for about 25 minutes or until the liquid has almost evaporated. Serve as a side dish. Any leftovers can be kept refrigerated for 3–4 days.

BRAISED SOYA BEANS

DAIZU NO AMA-NI

The humble soya bean is the most widely used ingredient in Japanese cuisine, forming the basis for soy sauce, *tofu* and *miso*. Soya beans are rich in nutrients and fibre and are regarded in Japan as 'meat from the earth'.

INGREDIENTS

3 dried shiitake mushrooms
7.5 cm (3 in) dried kelp, wiped with a damp cloth
420 g (15 oz) tinned soya beans, drained
50 g (2 oz) carrots, peeled and diced
2 tablespoons caster sugar
1½ tablespoons soy sauce

1 Soak the shiitake mushrooms and kelp in 200 ml (7 fl oz) of water for 30 minutes. Reserve the water. Dice the shiitake mushrooms and kelp into small pieces.

2 Put the kelp, mushrooms, and reserved water into a pan. Add the soya beans, carrot, an extra 100 ml (4 fl oz) of fresh water, and the sugar. Bring to the boil and cook, uncovered, for 15 minutes.

3 Add the soy sauce and simmer for a further 10 minutes. Serve as a side dish. Any leftovers can be stored in a fridge for up to a week.

CUCUMBER AND *WAKAME*

in Sweet and Sour Dressing

KYUURI TO WAKAME NO SANBAI-ZU

Although this is a cold dish, it is not regarded as a salad in Japan. If you can't get hold of rice vinegar, ordinary malt vinegar will do as a substitute.

INGREDIENTS

200 g (7 oz) cucumber, cut in half lengthways and then very thinly sliced

1 teaspoon salt

½ tablespoon dried wakame *soaked in hot water for a few minutes until swollen*

FOR THE SWEET AND SOUR DRESSING

5 teaspoons rice vinegar

½ tablespoon caster sugar

½ teaspoon soy sauce

❶ Put the cucumber in a bowl, sprinkle with the salt and leave for 15 minutes.

❷ Taking the cucumber in your hands, squeeze out as much liquid as you can. Do the same with the *wakame*.

❸ Mix together the sugar, vinegar and soy sauce in a small bowl.

❹ Just before eating, mix the dressing together with the cucumber and *wakame*. Serve as a side dish.

BASIC *SUSHI* RICE

SUSHI YO GOHAN

This is the basic technique for producing the glutinous, vinegar-flavoured rice that forms the basis of all the variants of *sushi*. Japanese short-grain rice is essential for making sushi rice. The ratio of Japanese rice to water should be 1 part rice to 1¼ parts water.

INGREDIENTS

165 g (5½ oz) Japanese short-grain rice
2.5 cm (1 in) strip dried kelp
250 ml (8 fl oz) water

FOR THE SUSHI-ZU

1½ tablespoons rice vinegar
1 tablespoon caster sugar
½ teaspoon salt

❶ Put the rice in a pan and rinse several times until the water is almost clear. Leave the rice in a sieve for 30 minutes so the individual grains can begin to absorb the water remaining in the sieve. Add the water, rice and kelp to a pan. Bring to the boil, taking the kelp out just before boiling point. Simmer, covered, for about 10 minutes. (Simmering time depends on the amount of rice you cook.)

❷ Test the rice to see if it has softened. Turn off the heat and leave for 10 minutes. Mix the vinegar, sugar and salt in a bowl. Put the rice in a large bowl. Wet the wooden spoon and add the *sushi-zu* a little at a time, 'cutting' it into the rice with the wooden spoon (not stirring or mashing), until you have used all the liquid. The rice will now be giving off the sharp aroma of the *sushi-zu*. Leave to cool before using.

"ROLL YOUR OWN" SUSHI

TEMAKI-ZUSHI

A modern and very popular variant on the *sushi* theme. *Temaki-zushi* makes a great change for dinner parties.

INGREDIENTS
1 quantity basic sushi *rice (see p. 60)*
5 sheets of nori, *each cut into 4 pieces*
5 diagonal slices of cucumber, cut into long matchsticks
¼ avocado, sliced
1 rollmop herring, sliced
1 bunch cress
Soy sauce

FOR THE FILLING
90 g (3½ oz) tuna in brine
1 tablespoon mayonnaise

FOR THE OMELETTE
1 egg
1 teaspoon caster sugar
A pinch of salt
2 teaspoons vegetable oil, for frying

❶ To prepare the filling, first drain the tuna and then mix with the mayonnaise. Make a Japanese style omelette (see p.52), which should be cut into strips after cooling down. Now lay all the ingredients out on a large serving plate. The rice is laid out on a separate plate as are the strips of *nori*.

❷ Each diner takes a piece of *nori* in one hand and scoops about a tablespoon of rice onto it, spreading it quite thinly.

❸ Next, a portion of one or a combination of the fillings are taken with *hashi* and laid in the centre of the sheet. Last, the diner rolls the *nori* into a cornet shape, dipping it into his or her small bowl of soy sauce before eating.

THIN ROLLS of Cucumber and Pickled Radish

HOSO-MAKI ZUSHI: KAPPA-MAKI AND TAKUWAN-MAKI

*K*appa-maki or cucumber rolls is made with narrow strips of the cucumber. *Takuwan*, made by a process of drying then pickling the Japanese giant radish or *dai-kon*, is used for *takuwan-maki*. These two *hoso-maki* could be called 'family sushi' as they are often made at home rather than being bought in.

INGREDIENTS

1 quantity basic sushi *rice (see p. 60)*
2.5 sheets nori, *cut into half*
1 cucumber
2 takuwan *sticks of 5 mm x 19 cm (¼ x 7½ in)*
2½ teaspoons toasted sesame seeds
A little wasabi *(optional)*

1 Cut the cucumber into 3 sticks each 5 mm x 19 cm (¼ x 7½ in).

2 Place the *nori* on a *sushi* mat or a chopping board covered with cling film or polythene. Spread the rice evenly on the nori, except for a 1.5 cm (¾ in) strip clear along the far edge. Using the tip of your finger, smooth a small amount of *wasabi* paste over the rice.

3 Place the cucumber sticks onto the rice and sprinkle over ½ teaspoon of toasted sesame seeds.

4 Roll over the *sushi* mat and form to shape. The *nori* is sealed by the moisture from the rice. In the same way, make 2 more *hoso-maki* with the cucumbers and make 2 with *takuwan*. Cut each roll into 5 pieces using a knife wetted with a mixture of water and vinegar to give a clean cut.

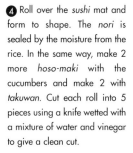

HOW TO CUT THE CUCUMBER AND TAKUWAN

With a sharp knife, pare a 5 mm (⅓ in) thick strip from the length of the cucumber. Next, slice down each side of the centre of the strip lengthways, so that you have three strips of roughly equal size. Prepare the takuwan in the same way.

LARGE *SUSHI* ROLLS

FUTO-MAKI ZUSHI

You might think it takes real skill and experience to produce good *futo-maki*, but after a couple of practice runs, you should get the hang of it. Nevertheless, well made *futo-maki* will undoubtedly impress your dinner guests.

INGREDIENTS

1 quantity basic sushi rice (see p. 60)
3 dried shiitake mushrooms, rinsed and soaked in 50 ml (2 fl oz) water
1 teaspoon caster sugar
1 tsp soy sauce
2 sheets nori seaweed sheets
6 seafood sticks
1 bunch cress

FOR THE OMELETTE

1 egg, beaten
1 teaspoon caster sugar
A pinch of salt
Vegetable oil, for frying

1 To prepare the filling, slice the mushrooms and put in a pan with the water they were soaked in, the caster sugar and the soy sauce. Bring this mixture to the boil and simmer for 5 minutes. Put the sugar and salt into a bowl with the beaten egg and mix together well. Heat the oil in an omelette pan and make a Japanese style omelette (see p.52). Let the omelette cool and then cut lengthways into three strips.

2 Place the *nori* squarely on a *sushi* mat or a chopping board covered with cling film. Spread the rice onto the *nori*, leaving a 2.5 cm (1 in) strip free of rice at the far edge.

3 Next, lay, in order half the omelette, shiitake, seafood sticks and cress in lines across the bed of rice, leaving a small strip of bare rice between each ingredient.

4 Now, holding the egg in place, pull the near edge of the *nori* sheet up and over in one motion until the *nori* has enfolded all the ingredients laid on the rice. Next, use your fingers to tuck the near edge of the *nori* inside the roll. Then, rotate the mat until the join is turned to the bottom of the roll.

5 Grip the far end of the *sushi* mat with your right hand and hold the roll with your left. Now, pull the roll firmly towards you to ensure that the *futo-maki* becomes well-packed. Finally, line up the sides of the mat by gently patting with the palms of your hands to clean up the ends of the roll. Gently unroll the mat to reveal the finished *futomaki* inside.

Repeat with the remaining half of the ingredients. When finished, slice the rolls into pieces the thickness of your thumb. Use a knife dipped in water mixed with vinegar so that the rice will not cling to the blade. Serve displayed on a large plate. The *futo-maki* should be taken from the plate and dipped into individual dishes of soy sauce before being eaten.

SALMON ROE *SUSHI*

IKURA-ZUSHI

Salmon roe is an expensive but popular ingredient in Japan. This dish makes a rather nice starter, although you can eat *Ikura-zushi* combined with rolled *sushi* or *Inari-zushi* as a main dish.

INGREDIENTS

4 tablespoons cooked sushi rice, see p.60
4 3.5 x 12.5 cm (1½ x 5 in) strips nori
2 slices cucumber, cut in half
4 teaspoons salmon roe

1 Wet your palm with a little water. Take 1 tablespoon of rice and form into a square-shaped ball. Make 3 other balls in the same way.

2 Place each rice ball in the middle of a strip of *nori*. Roll the *nori* around it, then stand it on a plate.

3 Place the sliced cucumber on top of each of the rice balls, and put 1 teaspoon of salmon roe on top of the cucumber. Serve with a dash of soy sauce.

FRIED BEAN CURD *SUSHI*

INARI-ZUSHI

These sweet-tasting sacks of *sushi* rice can be eaten along with other *sushi* dishes or alone as a tasty and filling snack. *Inari-zushi* also forms a part of many a Japanese picnic as well as being a firm favourite as a lunch box filler. Refer to the instructions for making basic *sushi* rice while cooking the rice.

INGREDIENTS

½ quantity of basic sushi rice (see p. 60)
2 sheets abura-age (thin bean curd)
120 ml (4 fl oz) dashi stock (see p. 13)
1½ tablespoons caster sugar
1 tablespoon mirin
2 teaspoons soy sauce
1 teaspoon toasted sesame seeds

❶ Gently roll the *abura-age*, using a chopstick as a rolling pin, to make it easier to handle. Place in a colander and rinse with hot water. Cut in half and gently open the 'sack'.

❷ Put the *dashi* stock, *mirin*, soy sauce and *abura-age* in a pan, bring to the boil and simmer for 20 minutes or until the *dashi* mixture has almost evaporated. Make a small lid with some aluminium foil and place on top of the *abura-age*. Continue to cook until the remaining liquid has been completely absorbed.

❸ Remove the *abura-age* and leave on a plate or chopping board until dry.

❹ Mix the *sushi* rice with the sesame and divide into 4 equal portions. Fill each *abura-age* with rice and fold to create a small sack.

JAPANESE RICE BALLS

ONIGIRI

*O*nigiri is a simply prepared and handy 'eat anytime' meal, that can be packed up in a picnic or served as an accompaniment at dinner. The use of the word 'ball' is slightly misleading as the shape of the finished product more closely resembles a triangle.

The use of Japanese rice for making rice balls is strongly recommended as other varieties tend to lack the characteristic stickiness of the Japanese grains.

INGREDIENTS

165 g (5½ oz) Japanese short-grain rice, rinsed well

A pinch of flaked bonito

¼ tablespoon soy sauce

1 Japanese pickled plum (ume-boshi), seeded and halved

4 strips 5 x 15 cm (2 x 6 in) nori

1 Rinse the rice until the water runs off almost clear.

2 Cook the rice the same way as making *sushi* rice (see p.60) but do not add the *sushi-zu*.

3 Let the rice cool down before use. Mix the *bonito* flakes with the soy sauce in a small saucer or plate to make a paste.

4 Wet and then sprinkle your palms with a little salt. (You will need to repeat this process with every ball you make.) Scoop up 3 heaped tablespoons of rice and mould it lightly into a round shape.

5 Once the rough ball shape is formed, make a small hole in the middle and put *either* half of the *bonito* paste or one half of the Japanese plum inside.

6 Cover the hole while at the same time trying to form the rice into a triangular shape.

7 When the 4 rice balls have been formed, wrap each with a strip of *nori*.

MIXED RICE

MAZE GOHAN

Japanese-style mixed rice is easy to make and can be served either as a main course with a soup and salad or instead of plain boiled rice to accompany other dishes.

INGREDIENTS

165 g (5½ oz) Japanese short-grain rice	1 tablespoon sugar
50 g (2 oz) carrot, peeled and cut into short matchsticks	1½ tablespoons soy sauce
3 shiitake mushrooms, cut into short matchsticks	3 mangetout
½ sheet abura-age, rinsed in hot water and cut into short matchsticks	A pinch of salt
1.5 cm (¼ in) piece koya dofu, soaked in water for 5 minutes, then cut into matchsticks	1 egg
	½ tablespoon water
135 ml (4½ fl oz) dashi stock (see p.13)	Vegetable oil, for frying
	2 red radishes, thinly sliced

1 First make *sushi* rice according to the instructions on p.60.

2 Put the carrots, shiitake, *abura-age*, *tofu*, dashi stock, sugar and soy sauce in a pan. Bring to the boil and simmer for 15 minutes.

3 Meanwhile, boil the mangetout in salted water for 3 minutes, then remove and cut finely on the slant.

4 Mix the egg, water and a pinch of salt together in a bowl. Heat the vegetable oil in an omelette pan and make 2 thin omelettes. Let the omelettes cool, then cut each one in half then slice it into thin strips.

5 When Step 2 is complete, mix the ingredients with the *sushi* rice. Place the rice mixture onto a large plate. Spread the egg, then the mangetout over the top and decorate with the radish and strips of *nori*.

CHICKEN AND EGG on Rice

OYAKO-DON

In Japan this dish is known as "parent and child on rice". The method of preparation ensures that the chicken is still tender and succulent when served. Long-grain rice can be used in this dish.

INGREDIENTS

165 g (5½ oz) short-grain rice
150 ml (5 fl oz) dashi stock (see p.13)
1 tablespoon caster sugar
1 tablespoon mirin
3 tablespoons soy sauce
2 boneless chicken breasts, diced
1 medium onion, sliced
1 egg, beaten
Watercress, for garnishing

1 Rinse and boil the rice according to the instructions on the packet.

2 Bring the *dashi* stock, sugar, *mirin* and soy sauce to the boil in a frying pan. Add the chicken and onion. Simmer for about 8 minutes or until the chicken is cooked.

3 Pour over the egg, letting it set on top of the chicken without stirring. When the egg has set, sprinkle on some watercress as a garnish. Serve the mixture on top of the serving of rice.

SUKIYAKI

SUKIYAKI

Sukiyaki is one of the few examples of Japanese cuisine to have become popular throughout the West. In Japan, a special, heavy pan is used, however *sukiyaki* can be prepared with any large, deep, frying pan. Like fondue, *sukiyaki* is always cooked at the table, diners taking food from the pan as soon as it is ready. The pan is then replenished from a plate of fresh meat and vegetables standing by, therefore there is no need for you to slave away in front of your cooker!

INGREDIENTS

2cm (1 in) cube of fresh beef suet or 1 tablespoon vegetable oil	200 g (7 oz) tofu, cut in half lengthwise and sliced
150 ml (5 fl oz) dashi stock (see p13)	300 g (10 oz) Chinese leaves, halved lengthwise and sliced
1½ tablespoons sugar	
2 tablespoons mirin	6 shiitake mushrooms, halved
1 tablespoon sake	1 short leek, sliced on a slant
2½ tablespoons soy sauce	300 g (10 oz) beef, sliced paper thin
1 medium onion, halved and sliced	2 raw eggs (optional)

❶ Heat the suet in a frying pan and add the *dashi* stock, sugar, *mirin*, sake and soy sauce. When this mixture begins to simmer, add half the amount of onions, *tofu*, Chinese leaves and shiitake, keeping each ingredient in its own separate group in the pan. Simmer for 7 minutes and then add half the beef placing it in the centre of the pan. Continue to simmer for several minutes until cooked.

❷ Break the raw eggs into 2 serving bowls and mix the yolk and white with your chopsticks. Take the cooked meat, *tofu* and vegetables a little at a time from the pan, dip them into the raw egg and eat with a bowl of rice. As the cooked ingredients are taken from the pan, replenish with the raw ingredients.

COD AND CHINESE Cabbage Pot

TARA TO HAKUSAI NO NABE

This very popular winter dish is normally cooked on the table using a portable gas or electric ring. Everyone at the table takes food from the pan, transferring it to their own, individual dishes while the hostess takes care to keep the pan stocked up with fresh raw ingredients. You will need a 20 cm (8 in) casserole dish.

INGREDIENTS

900 ml (1½ pints) water

7 cm (3 in) piece dried konbu, or kelp

1 small leek, sliced on a slant into 1 cm (½ in) widths

1 medium onion, sliced

2 x 300 g (10 oz) cod fillets or steaks, cut into large, bite-sized pieces

200 g (7 oz) Chinese leaves, cut in half lengthways and then sliced into 1 cm (½ in) strips

100 g (4 oz) momen or "cotton" tofu, cut into 1 cm (½ in) cubes

100 g (4 oz) carrots, peeled and thinly sliced

4 shiitake mushrooms, cut into halves

6 mangetout

FOR THE PONZU DRESSING

3 tablespoons soy sauce

1 tablespoon lemon juice

1 tablespoon vinegar

1 tablespoon mirin

½ tablespoon Japanese instant stock granules

FOR THE GARNISH

1 x 450 g (1 lb) mouli, peeled, grated and lightly squeezed

A pinch of seven spice or chilli pepper

1 Put the water and konbu in a flameproof casserole and bring to the boil. Add half the leek, onion, cod, Chinese leaves, tofu, carrots, shiitake mushrooms and mangetout, keeping groups together in the pan. Cook for 5–8 minutes, or until the vegetables are cooked.

2 Meanwhile, mix the soy sauce, lemon juice, vinegar, mirin and dashi stock granules in a jar and stir well.

3 When roughly half of the cooked food has been taken from the casserole, replenish with the raw ingredients.

TO SERVE

Put 2 tablespoons of mouli and 1 tablespoon ponzu dressing into each serving bowl.

As you take food from the casserole with your chopsticks, dip it into the dressing and eat. Add some seven spice if you wish to add a little more fire to the meal. As you eat, add more ponzu dressing and mouli when you need to. Serve with rice.

NOODLES in Soy Sauce Soup

SHOYU-RAMEN

*R*amen originally came from China but has been adapted to suit Japanese tastes. It is universally popular as a lunch dish or light meal. Once you make the *ramen* stock, it can be kept in the fridge for a few days or can be frozen. Topping for *ramen* varies. Melted butter and sweetcorn are one of the most popular choices. *Ramen* noodles are sold both dried and fresh. Cooking times for the two types are much the same, but dried noodles do, of course, keep longer once purchased.

INGREDIENTS

FOR THE BASIC *RAMEN* STOCK MAKES ABOUT 1.6 LITRES (2¾ PINTS)
280 g (10 oz) chicken carcass, roughly chopped
2 pork bones
½ leek
2.5 cm (1 in) piece root ginger, peeled and cut in half
1 large garlic clove, cut in half
2.25 litres (4 pints) water

FOR THE *SHOYU RAMEN*
250 g (9 oz) fresh ramen noodles
600 ml (1 pint) ramen stock
3 tablespoons soy sauce
½ teaspoon salt
A pinch of freshly ground black pepper

FOR THE TOPPING
8 tablespoons sweetcorn kernels
3 spring onions, chopped
20 g (¼ oz) butter, cut in half

1 To make the *ramen* stock, blanch the chicken and pork bones. Then put the water, bones, leek, ginger and garlic into a large pan. Bring to the boil and simmer for 1 hour, occasionally skimming off the scum. Strain the stock through a sieve. Adjust the heat to prevent the stock from boiling again (this will make the liquid cloudy).

2 Boil the noodles for about 2–2½ minutes. Drain and put them in individual bowls.

3 Heat the 600 ml (1 pint) of stock, soy sauce, salt and pepper in a pan. When it boils, pour the soup into the bowls. Put 4 tablespoons of the sweetcorn on top of the noodles, sprinkle with the chopped spring onion, then top with the butter. Eat as soon as possible or the noodles will absorb the soup and become soggy.

RAMEN NOODLES in Miso Soup

MISO RAMEN

Ramen is Japanese fast-food. In this variation, the flavour of fried garlic and sesame oil complements the *miso* and chilli. It is difficult not to make a noise when you eat Japanese noodles. In fact, the more you slurp, the better you will enjoy the meal, or so it is said!

INGREDIENTS

250 g (9 oz) fresh ramen *noodles*
600 ml (1 pint) ramen stock, (see p.74)
½ teaspoon salt
A pinch of freshly ground black pepper
2 teaspoons sesame oil
2 teaspoons toasted sesame seeds
3 tablespoons miso *paste*

FOR THE TOPPING

1 tablespoon sesame oil
175 g (6 oz) bean sprouts
1 large garlic clove, sliced
½ red pepper, thinly sliced
A pinch of chilli powder
A pinch of salt

1 Cook the noodles for about 2–2½ minutes in boiling water. Drain and put into the individual bowls.

2 Heat the stock and salt and pepper in a pan. When it boils, add the sesame oil and sesame seeds and stir in the *miso* paste until it has dissolved completely.

3 Meanwhile, heat the oil in a frying pan. Stir-fry the bean sprouts, garlic and red pepper. Sprinkle in the pinch of chilli pepper and salt. Place the vegetables on top of the noodles. Pour over the *miso* soup, serve and eat immediately.

BUCKWHEAT Noodles Topped with Deep-fried King Prawn

TEMPURA SOBA

oba noodles are made from buckwheat and are distinguished by their brown colour. Like *ramen* noodles, they can be bought fresh or dried. *Soba* is considered to be a very healthy food by the Japanese, and topping a dish of the noodles with a king prawn turns a nourishing meal into a gourmet experience.

INGREDIENTS

2 *king* or *tiger* prawns

A little plain flour

4 shiitake mushrooms

150 g (5 oz) dried soba

FOR THE BATTER

2 tablespoons plain flour

½ egg, beaten

4 tablespoons water

FOR THE SOUP

600 ml (1 pint) dashi stock (see p. 13)

1 teaspoon salt

2 teaspoons caster sugar

2 tablespoons mirin

2 tablespoons soy sauce

2 spring onions, chopped

1 To make the topping mix the flour, egg and water lightly in a bowl. Coat the prawns with flour and dip in the batter. Dip the mushrooms into the batter. Heat the oil to 180°C/350°F and deep fry until light golden brown.

2 Bring a large pan of water to the boil. Add the *soba* and cook for about 3 minutes. Briefly rinse with cold water and then drain. Divide the *soba* equally between two bowls.

3 Put the *dashi* stock, salt, sugar, *mirin* and soy sauce in a pan and bring to the boil. Add to the bowls of *soba*.

4 Place one prawn and two mushrooms on the top of each bowl and sprinkle with chopped spring onion. Serve immediately.

WHEATFLOUR Noodles with Egg

KAKITAMA-UDON

*U*don is the name given by the Japanese to those noodles made from wheatflour. A great favourite in the winter months because of its warming properties, *udon* comes in various shapes, some flat, some round in section, some as thick as a little finger, others as thin as spaghetti.

INGREDIENTS

300 g (10 oz) fresh udon
FOR THE SOUP
600 ml (1 pint) dashi *stock (see p.13)*
1 teaspoon salt
2 teaspoons caster sugar
2 tablespoons mirin
2 tablespoons soy sauce
1 egg, beaten
2 teaspoons cornflour
2 teaspoons water
2 spring onions, chopped

1 Bring a large pan of water to the boil. Add the *udon* and boil for 2 minutes. Drain and then place in equal portions into the 2 bowls.

2 Put the *dashi*, salt, sugar, *mirin* and soy sauce in a pan and bring to the boil. Pour ⅔ of the liquid into the 2 bowls. Bring the remainder back to the boil and gradually add the egg, mixing lightly so that when the egg rises to the surface, it is cooked in fronds.

3 Mix the cornflour and water into a paste and then add this to the soup to thicken. Pour the egg mixture into the bowls. Sprinkle with the spring onion and serve immediately.

GLOSSARY

Abura-age Deep fried thin beancurd, usually sliced and used as a garnish or slit into a pocket and stuffed with rice. *Abura-age* can be frozen but does not keep longer than 48 hours refrigerated.

Dried shiitake The most common mushroom used in Japanese cookery, its taste and texture differs significantly from other types. If bought dried, soak in water for at least 30 minutes prior to use. The water can be reserved for later use in *dashi*.

Konbu *Konbu* or kelp is one of the best sources of iodine available and also contains several other important minerals. Care should be taken not to over-boil *konbu* as it very quickly becomes bitter. Wipe to prepare *konbu* for cooking but do not rinse, as this will wash away many of the nutrients.

Koya dofu Freeze-dried *tofu* which will keep for up to 6 months in its dried form. To prepare for use,

soak in water until the *tofu* has swollen and become spongy.

Mirin Japanese cooking wine, though with only a trace of alcohol. This syrupy rice derivative imparts a distinctive sweet flavour to the dishes in which it is used.

Miso This is made from fermenting cooked soya beans with a Japanese type of yeast known as *koji*. *Miso* is unique to Japanese cuisine and widely used both as a flavouring and as the basis for dressings. It is rich in protein. Kept refrigerated, it will last for several months. There are two common types: white *miso* (made from a rice-based yeast) and red *miso* (made from a barley yeast). White *miso* is more commonly used in soups while the red type finds favour as a general purpose flavouring and for dishes where a richer flavour is desired.

Nori The most widely used seaweed, sold in

paper-thin sheets. Before use, *nori* is toasted quickly under a grill or over a gas ring until the colour changes from an almost inky black to dark green. Some pre-toasted *nori* is available, so take care to check which sort you are buying.

Rice vinegar Known as *su*, Japanese rice vinegar is made from naturally fermented rice. Clear *su* is common and suitable for *sushi* rice. Brown *su*, which is the unrefined basis for white *su*, can be used in any recipe where the colour of the vinegar is not important to the final dish.

Sake Japanese rice wine, made all over Japan as well as in the United States. Unlike Western cooking, *sake* is only used sparingly in Japanese cookery. *Sake* is now widely available in the West, but if you cannot get it, you can use dry sherry instead.

Soy sauce Ubiquitous to Japanese cookery, this combination of fermented

GLOSSARY

soya beans, wheat and salt is a lighter, sweeter solution than Chinese soy. Japanese brands such as Kikkoman are now widely available.

Wakame A seaweed typically used in Japanese soups and salads. *Wakame* can be used after simply dipping into boiling water. *Wakame* should never be cooked for long. It can be bought dried, in which case soaking for 5 minutes in cold water will make it ready for any cooking application.

Wasabi Misleadingly translated as 'horseradish', *wasabi* is ground from the *Wasabia japanica*, a Japanese riverside plant. Like English mustard, *wasabi* can be bought ready made, or in powder form to be mixed with a little water. Powdered *wasabi* is better than the ready-made variety, which tends to lose its "bite" fairly quickly.

INDEX